'Idea' Necklace

see photo on page 2

SIZE: Necklace 23", Pendant 2½" x 3½"

MATERIALS:

idea-ology Trinkets: Clear Fragments, Word Tag, Ornate Plate, Jump Rings, Link Chain
Scrapbook papers
Drill, Wire cutters
Ranger Glossy Accents, E6000

INSTRUCTIONS:

1. Squirt a drop of Glossy Accents onto the back of each fragment. Place fragment onto paper. Let dry. Cut paper around the fragment.
2. Cut top section from ornate plate and adhere to a fragment.
3. Assemble fragments in layers as shown and glue together.
4. Drill a hole in the upper right and left corners of the pendant.
5. Adhere washer to pendant.
6. Attach each end of chain to pendant with a jump ring.

Apply Glossy Accents: Apply Glossy Accents to the back of each Clear Fragment.

Adhere to Fragment: Place fragment onto paper. Let dry. Cut paper from the edges.

'Artful' Necklace

SIZE: Necklace 16½", Pendant 3¾"

MATERIALS:

idea-ology Trinkets: Clear square Fragment, Word Tag, 2 Hinge Clips, Jump Rings, Toggle clasp
Scrapbook paper, *Ranger* Glossy Accents
Flexible beading wire, Crimp beads, Crimp bead covers, Beads
Rubber Stamp, *Stamp Page* Pigment ink

INSTRUCTIONS:

1. Adhere paper to the back of the fragment with Glossy Accents.
2. Stamp an image on the front of the fragment.
3. Attach 2 hinge clips.
4. On the bottom hinge clip, add jump ring and word tag.
5. Fold beading thread in half. Thread fold of beading wire through "back" hole of top hinge clip to make a Lark's Head knot.
6. String beads on each side.
7. Finish with a crimp bead, crimp bead cover, and toggle clasp.

Mini Paper Clip Necklace

SIZE: Necklace 29", Pendant 1½"

MATERIALS:

idea-ology Trinkets: 48 Mini Paper Clips, Word Token
Red seed beads
Bead thread, beading needle

INSTRUCTIONS:

1. Slide a seed bead on each paper clip.
2. Connect paper clips to form a chain.
3. String 7 seed beads on bead thread. Thread bead string through word token and the center paper clip. Tightly knot the bead thread.

Fragments of Color

SIZE: 16$\frac{3}{4}$"

MATERIALS:

idea-ology Trinkets: 8 Clear Fragments,
Small Swivel Clasp, 8 Jump Rings
16$\frac{3}{4}$" Link Chain

Scrapbook paper

Ranger Glossy Accents

INSTRUCTIONS:

1. Squeeze a bit of Glossy Accents on fragment and place on paper, swirling it around for even coverage. Let dry.
2. Cut paper around edge of fragment.
3. Attach fragments to chain with jump rings.
4. Attach clasp to 1 end of the chain.

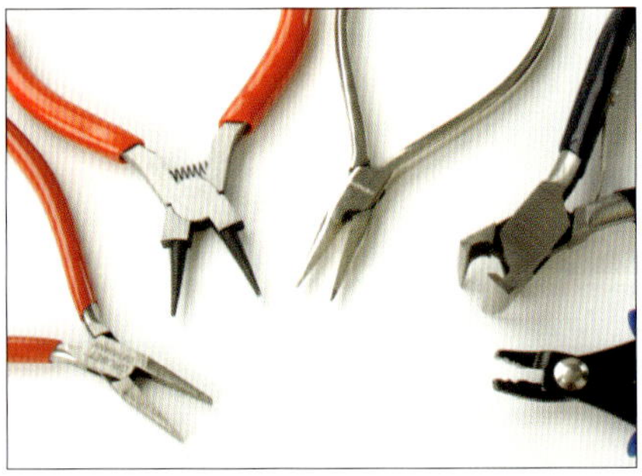

Basic Tools:
Needle-nose pliers, Round-nose pliers, Chain-nose pliers, End nippers, Crimp pliers

Basic Stringing Supplies:
Beading wire, Toggle clasp, Crimp beads

Adhere Fragments to Paper:
Squeeze a drop of Glossy Accents glue on the back of a clear plastic fragment. Place the fragment, glue side down, onto decorative scrapbook paper or a photo. Swirl around until coverage of glue is complete. Let dry. Cut around fragment with scissors.

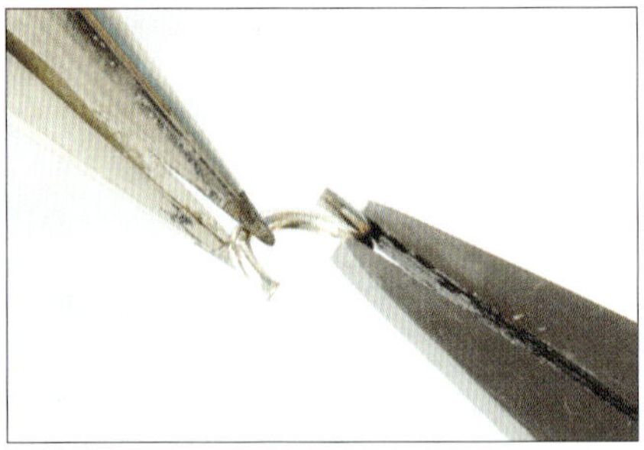

How to Close a Jump Ring:
Grasp the ring on each side of the opening with pliers. Twist sideways rather than pulling it open.

Necklace & Bracelet Clasps:
The projects in this book use two different types of clasp, the Toggle clasp (pictured first) is the most common. The Lobster Claw clasp is often used with a jump ring.

Sprocket Gear Necklace

SIZE: 26½"

MATERIALS:
idea-ology Trinkets: 18" Link Chain, Toggle Clasp, Jump Rings, 13 Sprocket Gears
22 gauge wire (Copper, Black)
6 strips leather ¼" x 4"
11 Silver 2" head pins
11 beads

INSTRUCTIONS:
1. Cut 2 pieces of 7-link chain and attach a section of the clasp to each piece with a jump ring.
2. Cut 6 pieces of 3-link chain. Add a sprocket gear to each end with a jump ring.
3. Wire wrap 3 gears and use them to connect the sprocket gear sections.
4. Insert a head pin into each bead and attach to a link between sprocket gears with a wrapped loop.
5. Tie a leather strip on each 3-link chain.

Game Spinner Earrings

SIZE: 2¼"

MATERIALS:
idea-ology Trinkets: Game Spinners: 2 large, 2 small, 2 Brass mini brads
2 Earring wires
Drill

INSTRUCTIONS:
1. Drill holes in top of large game spinners.
2. Attach large spinners to earring wires.
3. Attach small spinners to large spinners with brads.

Necklaces

Versatility is the name of the game when working with idea-ology trinkets. These examples illustrate the range of possibilities. From dressed-up crystal elegance to industrial strength, these pieces possess unique personality.

Key to My Heart Necklace

SIZE: 19"

MATERIALS:
idea-ology Trinkets: Key, Keyhole, Toggle Clasp, Jump Rings
22 gauge wire
Flexible Beading Wire
Heart beads, Spacer beads, Crimp beads

INSTRUCTIONS:
1. With 22 gauge wire, create a wrapped loop around each end of key.
2. Attach keyhole to key with 3 jump rings.
3. Attach beading wire to key with a crimp bead.
4. String 9" of beads on each side and attach to clasp with a crimp bead.

Key to the Birdhouse

This home will be rented for a song; keys provided for life. Make a statement with a pendant that sings of those things that matter most.

SIZE: Necklace: 18", Pendant: 1¼" x 3½"

MATERIALS:
idea-ology Trinkets: Ball chain and Connector
Metal Frame Corner, Keyhole, Key
2 Jump Rings
Ranger: 1" x 1" metal Frame
2 glass 1" x 1" slides
Green leaf bead, Head pin, Rhinestone
1" x 1" Bird image
E6000 glue

INSTRUCTIONS:
1. Sandwich bird image between glass slides.
2. Insert glass slides into frame.
3. Glue metal corner to top of frame.
4. Adhere rhinestone.
5. Insert head pin into leaf bead and create a dangle with a wrapped loop at the top.
6. Attach Keyhole and leaf dangle to the bottom of the frame with a jump ring.
7. Attach key to the bottom hole of the keyhole with a jump ring.
8. Slip ball chain through top ring in frame and attach connector.

Stained Glass Bracelet

SIZE: 7¾"

MATERIALS:
idea-ology Trinkets: 5 Jump Rings
Ranger: 4 metal 1" x 1" Frames, 8 glass 1" x 1" slides
Adirondack Alcohol Inks
Silver Lobster Claw clasp

INSTRUCTIONS:
1. Drip ink onto each glass square as desired.
2. Place glass squares into frames.
3. Connect frames with jump rings.
4. Attach clasp with a jump ring.

Alcohol Ink on Glass:
Drop colors of ink onto each glass piece.

Add the Metal Frame:
Place glass pieces into frames.

Stained Glass Pendant

SIZE: Necklace: 16½", Pendant: 1" x 3"

MATERIALS:

idea-ology Trinkets: Link Chain, Toggle Clasp, Jump Ring
Ranger: Adirondack alcohol inks, 2 glass 1" x 3" slides
Solder with Scalloped Edge, Copper tape, Flux
1" x 3" scrapbook paper, cotton swabs

INSTRUCTIONS:

1. Apply a light coating of ink to a piece of glass with a swab.
2. Squeeze 2 small drops of ink on same glass (see page 6).
3. Sandwich paper between the two slides.
4. Place Copper tape around all sides. Add flux and solder.
5. Solder jump ring to top of pendant.
6. Thread chain through pendant and attach clasps.

Birdhouse Pendant

SIZE: Necklace: 18", Pendant: 1½" x 3½"

MATERIALS:

idea-ology Trinkets: Metal Frame Corner, 2 Foliage Flowers, Bead Chain and Toggle, Jump Ring
Ranger: 2 glass 1" x 3" slides, 1" x 3" Silver frame
Pigment ink, Embossing powder, Stamp
3 rhinestones, 1" x 3" scrapbook paper, Drill, E6000 glue

INSTRUCTIONS:

1. Drill hole into top corner of metal frame corner; attach jump ring.
2. Stamp image onto glass, apply embossing powder and heat set.
3. Place paper between glass slides and place slides into frame.
4. Glue Corner, flowers, and rhinestones in place.
5. Thread ball chain through jump ring and attach toggle.

Ornate Bracelet

Capture the beauty of old style name plates and photo pendants with this fabulous bracelet. Personalize this project with a photo or paper to match your favorite outfit.

SIZE: 8"

MATERIALS:

idea-ology Trinkets:
- Ornate Plate
- Two $2\frac{3}{4}$" Swivel Clasps

Scrapbook paper

Ranger Glossy Accents

INSTRUCTIONS:

1. Cut plastic from frame packaging to fit into frame opening.
2. Use plastic as a stencil to cut scrapbook paper.
3. Glue paper to plastic with Glossy Accents and adhere to frame.
4. Attach a clasp to each side of the frame.

Ornate Frame Pendant

Vintage Victorian is all the rage and this pendant carries the weight and style of an elegant past into the twenty-first century.

The combination of metals makes this a great accessory for everything from a black t-shirt to a Gibson Girl silk blouse.

SIZE: Necklace: 20", Pendant: $2\frac{3}{4}$" x $4\frac{1}{4}$"

MATERIALS:

idea-ology Trinkets:
- Swivel Clasps (Two $2\frac{3}{4}$", Four $3\frac{3}{4}$")
- Ornate Frame
- Key
- Trinket Pin
- 1 Jump Ring

Ranger Glossy Accents

Scrapbook Paper

INSTRUCTIONS:

1. Cut plastic from frame packaging to fit into frame opening.
2. Use plastic as a stencil to cut scrapbook paper.
3. Glue paper to plastic with Glossy Accents and adhere to frame.
4. Attach key and trinket pin with jump ring.
5. On each side of the frame, attach 2 large Swivel Clasps, ending with 1 small clasp.

Arrow Pendant

Do you feel like your life is going in circles? Perhaps this attractive pendant will provide some direction in your day.

SIZE: Necklace 20", Pendant 2" x 2½"

MATERIALS:

idea-ology Trinkets: Arrow from Grungeboard Mixed Minis Plain
Ranger Adirondack Alcohol inks
Two 10" Silver chains, 2 Silver eyelets, Silver toggle clasp, 4 Silver jump rings
Hole punch, Eyelet tools, Cotton swab

INSTRUCTIONS:

1. Color Grungeboard with alcohol inks.
2. Punch holes in Grungeboard arrow and set eyelets.
3. Open jump rings, thread through eyelets and attach chain.
4. Add clasp to chain with jump rings.

Alcohol Ink on Board: Squeeze 2 - 3 drops of alcohol ink onto a cotton swab. Rub alcohol ink onto Grungeboard.

Apply Mixatives: Add metallic "mixatives" to the surface to increase depth and enhance the colors.

Butterfly Pins

Nothing picks up your day like wearing one-of-a-kind jewelry - especially when it doubles as such interesting, eye-catching art. These pretty pins will flutter most fittingly into a gift box too.

SIZE: 2½" x 3"

MATERIALS:

idea-ology Trinkets: Butterfly shapes from Grungeboard Nature Swirls, Large Game Spinner, Mini brads, Word Tags, Swivel Clasps
Ranger Distressed inks
Pin back, Hole punch
E6000

INSTRUCTIONS:

1. Color butterfly with inks.
2. Punch hole in center and attach spinner to front and jump ring end of swivel clasp to back with a brad.
3. Glue pin on back.
4. Attach word tag to swivel clasp.

'Wish' Bracelet

SIZE: 8"

MATERIALS:

idea-ology Trinkets: Link Chain and Toggle Clasp, Grungeboard (Basics Plain, Alphas Plain)
Ranger: Adirondack Alcohol Inks, Stickles Glitter glue
Eyelets, Hole punch, Eyelet Tools
Wire cutters, Jewelry pliers
Tacky glue

INSTRUCTIONS:

1. Cut a Grungeboard rectangle 3/4" x 3 5/8".
2. Color Grungeboard pieces with alcohol inks.
3. Highlight letters with Stickles. Let dry.
4. Glue letters to rectangle. Let dry.
5. Punch holes and insert eyelets on both ends of rectangle.
6. Cut two 5-link sections of chain. Open a link, pass through eyelet and close link.
7. Attach clasps to 5-link sections.

Flower Bracelet

SIZE: 7"

MATERIALS:

idea-ology Trinkets: Oval from Grungeboard Mixed Minis Plain
Foliage: 1" Flower, 1" Leaf, 1 Brad
6 Jump Rings, 1 Toggle Clasp
Ranger Adirondack Alcohol Inks
2 Eyelets, Hole punch, Eyelet tools
Leather lacing, Leather Crimps

INSTRUCTIONS:

1. Color Grungeboard oval with alcohol inks.
2. Punch holes and set eyelets at both ends of oval.
3. Punch hole in center of oval and attach foliage with a brad.
4. Insert leather lacing through eyelet and fold lace in half.
5. Slide 2 jump rings over doubled lace on each side.
6. Attach leather crimps.
7. Attach clasps to leather crimps.

Circles Bracelet

Encircle your wrist with the look of old leather. This bracelet is the perfect complement for your jeans and cowboy boots.

SIZE: 8"

MATERIALS:

idea-ology Trinkets:
12 Copper Jump Rings
6 circles from Grungeboard Shapes Plain
6 stars from Grungeboard Minis Plain
Ranger Adirondack Alcohol inks
12 Copper eyelets
6 Silver 1/8" jump rings
Silver Lobster Claw clasp
Cotton swabs, Hole punch, Eyelet tools

INSTRUCTIONS:

1. Using cotton swab, paint Grungeboard shapes with alcohol inks.
2. Punch holes and set eyelets.
3. Attach 3 jump rings Copper-Silver-Copper between each circle.
4. Attach the clasp to one end with a Silver jump ring.

Treasure Necklace

SIZE: 23"

MATERIALS:

idea-ology Trinkets: Link Chain with Toggle Clasp, Brass Brad, Word Tag, Swivel Clasp, Small Game Spinner, Mini paper clip, 3 Keys, Ornate Plate, Wish Ticket, 2 Key Holes, 2 Word Tokens, Clear Fragments, 2 Stencil Type letters, 4 Trinket Pins, 2 Hinge Clips, 26 Jump Rings
Assorted beads, 14 head pins, 2 eye pins, 20 gauge wire
Bird charms, Flower brad
Scrapbook paper
Ranger: Adirondack Alcohol Inks (Lettuce, Cranberry) Glossy Accents
GS Hypo Cement

INSTRUCTIONS:

1. Attach clasps to link chain.
2. Make 16 bead dangles using head pins, eye pins, and charms.
3. Attach trinkets to chain with jump rings.
4. Drip Glossy Accents on back of fragments. Adhere to paper and cut out. Drill a hole in 1 fragment, add flower brad. Attach hinge clip. Color bird charm with alcohol inks and cement to 1 fragment. Attach fragments & hinge clips to chain with jump rings.
5. Cut plastic from Ornate Plate packaging to fit opening on the plate. Adhere "ticket" with glossy accents. Attach bead dangle to bottom with a jump ring.
6. Attach small spinner to keyhole with brad.
7. Attach all charms to chain links as desired.

How to Make a Beaded Dangle

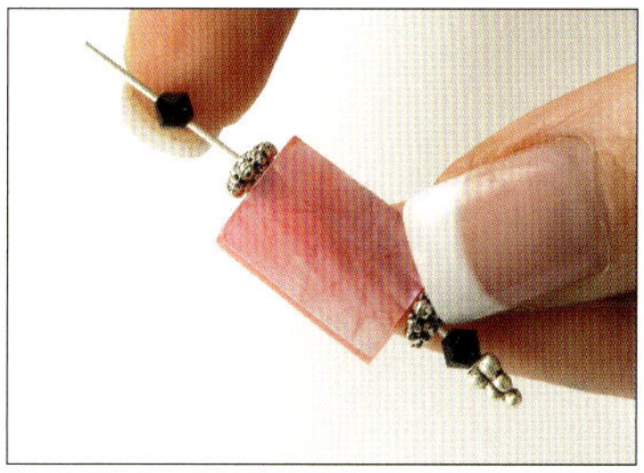

String Beads: 1. String beads onto a head pin.

Make an Angle: 2. Use flat-nose pliers to bend a right angle in the head pin.

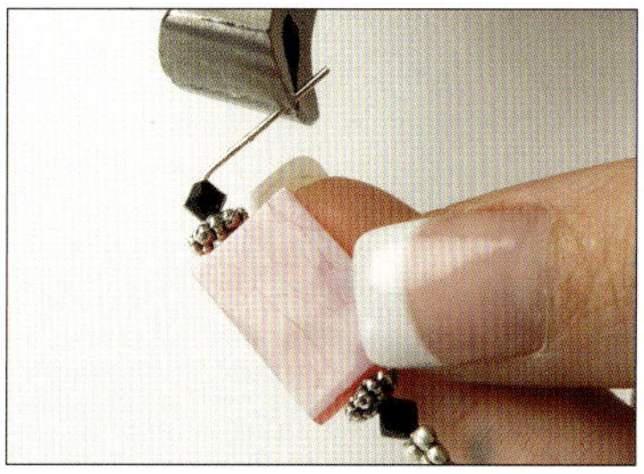

Trim the End: 3. Trim the end.

Turn a Loop: 4. Turn a loop using round-nose pliers.

Earrings

for all occasions

Gears & Leaves

SIZE: 2"

MATERIALS:

idea-ology Trinkets:
Two ¾" Gears, 2 Brads
Two ⅞" Foliage Leaves
Two ⅜" Foliage Flowers
4 Jump Rings
2 Earring Wires

INSTRUCTIONS:
1. Layer foliage with a brad.
2. Insert a jump ring into the same hole as the brad and attach to gear.
3. Attach to earring wires with jump rings.

Attach Flower: Attach flower to gear with a jump ring.

Flower Power

SIZE: 1¼"

MATERIALS:

idea-ology Trinkets:
2 Clear Fragments
2 Jump Rings
Ranger Glossy Accents
2 Earring Wires
Double-sided scrapbook paper

INSTRUCTIONS:
1. Apply Glossy Accents to back of fragments and adhere to paper. Let dry. Cut out around fragment.
2. Attach to ear wires with jump ring.
Tip: Using double-sided paper gives the back of the earring a finished look.

Add Paper to Fragment: Squeeze Glossy Accents onto the back of the fragment and place on paper before cutting.

'L' Token

SIZE: 1½"

MATERIALS:

idea-ology Trinkets:
2 Word Tokens
2 Beads, 22 gauge wire
2 Earring Wires

INSTRUCTIONS:
Wire wrap bead between word token and earring wire.

Wrap Wire: Wire wrap bead between word token and earring wire.

Sunburst

SIZE: 1¾"

MATERIALS:

idea-ology Trinkets:
2 Clear Fragments
2 Jump Rings
Ranger: Glossy Accents
Stickles glitter glue
2 Earring Wires
Double-sided scrapbook paper

INSTRUCTIONS:
1. Apply Glossy Accents to back of fragments and adhere to paper. Let dry. Cut out around fragment.
2. Apply Stickles to front of fragment.
3. Attach earring wires with jump rings.

Apply Stickles: Apply Distressed Stickles to the surface of the fragment.

Layered Gears

SIZE: 1"

MATERIALS:

idea-ology Trinkets:
Two ⅞" wheel Gears
Two ¾" Sprocket Gears
Two ⅜" Foliage flowers
2 Brads, 2 Jump Rings
2 Earring Wires

INSTRUCTIONS:
1. Layer flower-gear-sprocket and secure with a brad.
2. Attach each earring wire with jump ring.

Layer Gears: Assemble flower, gear, and sprocket with a brad.

Bead Dangles

SIZE: 1"

MATERIALS:

idea-ology Trinkets:
Two ⅞" Sprocket Gears
2 Jump Rings
2 Beads, 2 Head pins
2 Earring Wires

INSTRUCTIONS:
1. String each bead on a head pin and make a wrapped loop.
2. Attach bead and gear to earring wire with a jump ring.

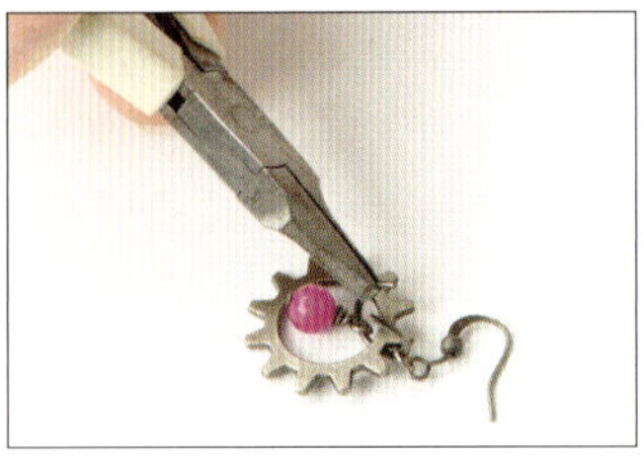

Attaching Parts: Attach bead dangle and gear to ear wire with a jump ring.

Trinket Dangles

SIZE: 2¼"

MATERIALS:

idea-ology Trinkets:
Two 1" Wheel Gears
2 Trinket Pins
2 Jump Rings
2 Earring Wires

INSTRUCTIONS:
1. Attach pin to gear with a jump ring.
2. Attach each ear wire to gear.

Add Ear Wire: Open ear wire and thread onto gear.

Hearts

SIZE: 1"

MATERIALS:

idea-ology Trinkets:
Hearts from Grungeboard
Seasonal Swirls
2 Jump Rings
2 Copper eyelets
Ranger Adirondack Alcohol inks
Hole Punch/Eyelet Setter
2 Earring Wires, Cotton swab

INSTRUCTIONS:
1. Color hearts with inks.
2. Punch holes and set eyelets.
3. Attach to earring wires with jump rings.

Inking Grungeboard: Color hearts with alcohol inks.

Wrapped Gears

SIZE: 1⅜"

MATERIALS:

idea-ology Trinkets:
Two ¾" Sprocket Gears
2 Jump Rings
20 gauge wire
2 Earring Wires

INSTRUCTIONS:
1. Cut 2 wires 4" long.
2. Curl 1" on each end into a tight, flat spiral.
3. Fold each wire in half and form a small loop like the end of a safety pin.
4. Sandwich a gear between the spirals of 1 wire. Thread a jump ring through the center of the spiral, gear, and the spiral on the back. Repeat for remaining wire and gear.
5. Attach an earring wire through the center loop of each wire.

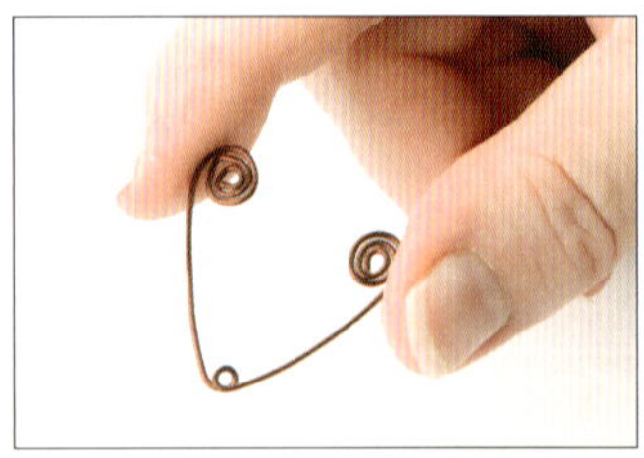

Shaping the Wire: Fold the wire in the middle, aligning the spirals and form a loop like the end of a safety pin.

Earrings

Earrings are the perfect accessory for every day and are suitable for all occasions. Express your personality with a unique collection of eye-catching earrings without spending a fortune. You'll love making these quick and easy projects and they are wonderful gifts.

Floral Bracelet

Smooth as silk against your wrist, this bead cuff presents an elegant bouquet of flowers that never fade.

SIZE: 3/4" x 7 1/4"

MATERIALS:
idea-ology Trinkets: Flowers and Leaves from the Foliage Collection
Size 8 Copper hex beads
Size 11 Gold seed beads
9 Pearls
Wildfire stringing thread, Beading needle

INSTRUCTIONS:
1. Create a bracelet cuff with hex beads using Peyote stitch.
2. Finish with a loop on onc end and a flower on the other for the closure.
3. Attach flowers with pearls by running thread through the rows.
4. Ribbon Bracelet option: Use 8" of grosgrain 3/4" wide ribbon as the base for the bracelet.

Bracelet Cuff:
Use a length of beaded bracelet (pictured) or grosgrain ribbon as the base for the bracelet.

Add a Clasp on Each End:
Finish with a loop on one end and a flower on the other for the closure.

Attach Flowers and Beads:
Attach flowers and pearls with thread.

Flat Peyote - Even Count

TIP: If you are learning this stitch, you may want to make a small practice swatch.

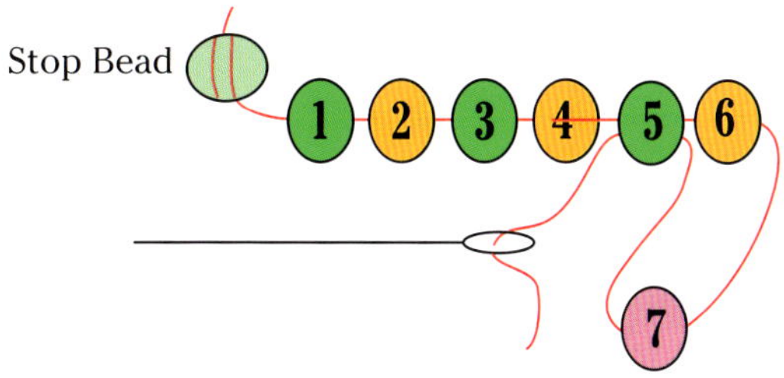

ROWS 1 AND 2 - String on 6 beads, using a "stop" bead about 8" from the end of the thread. Use a different size or style bead for the "stop" bead, so you will not confuse it with the others. Alternate colors of beads, as shown in the diagram. You can see on the diagrams that bead #1 would need to be the color of the beads you want in Row 2.

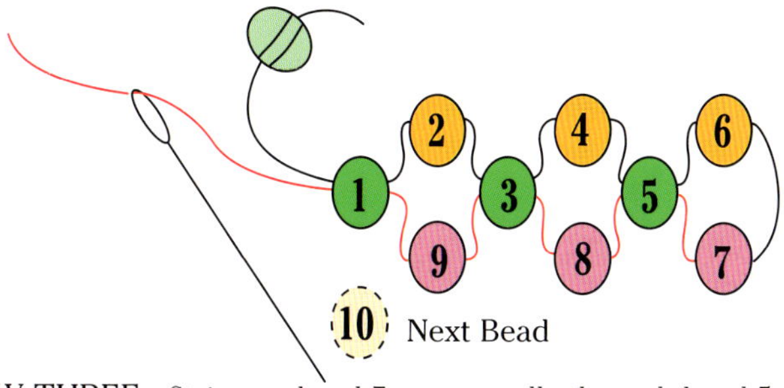

ROW THREE - String on bead 7, pass needle through bead 5. (You are "skipping" 6, the last bead strung.) Continue to add beads 8 - 9.

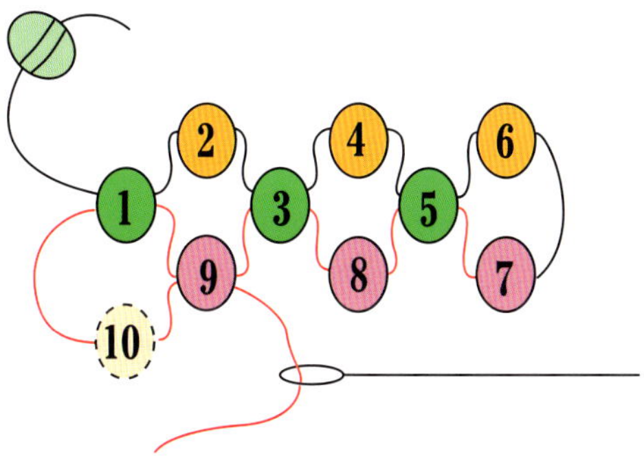

ROW FOUR - Add bead 10, pass needle through bead 9. Tip: Hold the work carefully at this point, as you do not want the beads to twist out of position. Your pattern would not be correct, and the twisted rows could cause problems with the tension. Continue adding beads 11 through 12. Bead 12 is the last bead on Row four.

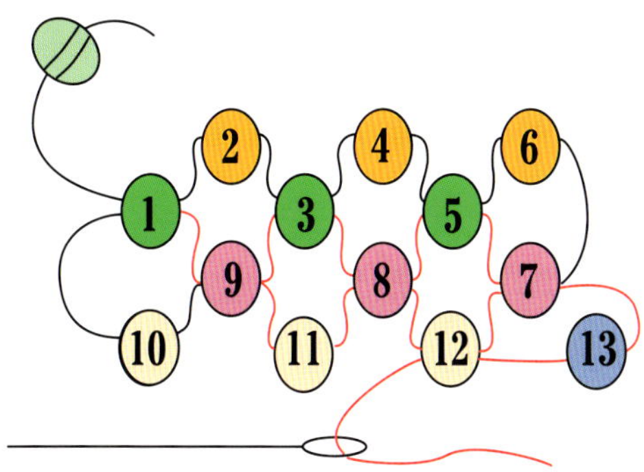

ROW FIVE - Add bead 13, passing needle through bead 12. Bead 13 is the first bead of Row five. As you add the rest of the beads in Row five, you will begin to see how the rows line up with each other, and how the beads fit into each other, like a zipper's teeth. You will have "down" beads that you go into when adding the next row. If you are using cylinder beads, this will be even more apparent.

'Journey' Necklace

Trinkets can express emotion and purpose as well as providing decoration. The game spinner points the direction of this artistic journey - perhaps it is a dream seen through a keyhole; with hopes pinned along the links of a life.

SIZE: Necklace: 19"
Pendant: $2\frac{1}{4}$" x $2\frac{3}{4}$"

MATERIALS:
idea-ology Trinkets: Word Tag, Keyhole,
Large Game Spinner, 6 Trinket Pins
Link Chain and Toggle Clasp
9 Jump Rings

INSTRUCTIONS:
1. Pendant: Attach a word tag to a game spinner with a jump ring.
2. Attach game spinner to keyhole with jump ring.
3. Attach pendant to center of chain with a jump ring.
4. Attach each trinket pin to chain with a jump ring.
5. Attach clasp.

Attach Word Tag: Attach a word tag to a game spinner with a jump ring.

Attach Pins: Attach each trinket pin to chain with a jump ring.

Attach a Clasp: Attach a toggle clasp to each end of the chain with a jump ring.

Rainbow Necklace

Some jewelry is just meant to be fun. Catch a rainbow of joy with an ensemble guaranteed to brighten your day.

SIZE: 19"

MATERIALS:
idea-ology Trinkets: Link Chain with Toggle Clasp,
38 Jump Rings, 38 Mini Safety Pins
152 size 11 seed beads

INSTRUCTIONS:
1. Lay out 38 safety pins and 38 jump rings.
2. Place 4 seed beads on each safety pin.
3. Attach safety pins to each link of chain using a jump ring.

Rainbow Earrings

SIZE: 1¼"
idea-ology Trinkets: 6 Mini Safety Pins
2 Eye pins, 2 Earring wires
34 size 11 seed beads

INSTRUCTIONS:
1. Prepare 6 safety pins as above.
2. Open eye pins. Place 5 seed beads on each, then secure 3 safety pins on each.
3. Wire wrap each safety pin to an earring wire.

Add Beads to Safety Pins: Place 4 seed beads on each safety pin.

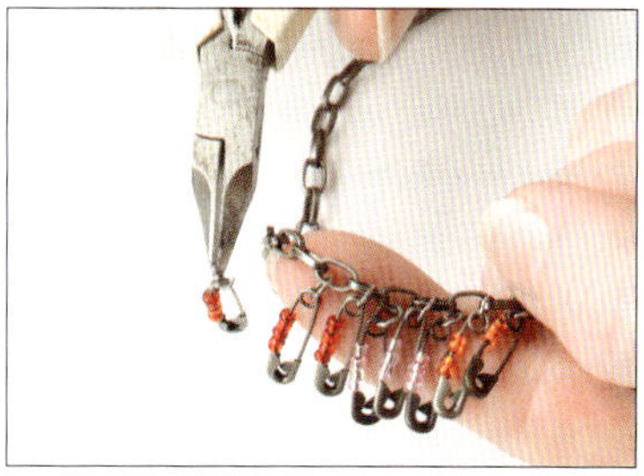

Attach Pins to Necklace: Attach a safety pin to each link of chain using a jump ring.

Add a Necklace Clasp: Attach a toggle clasp to each end of the necklace chain.

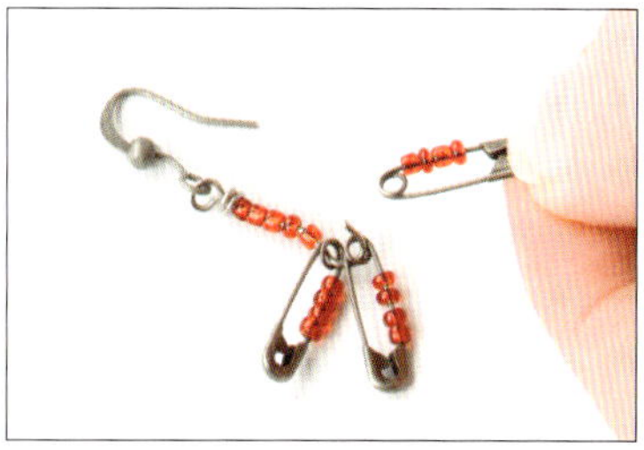

Earrings: Open eye pins and secure 3 safety pins on each eye pin.

'Simplify' Pin

Remind yourself to lighten your cares by simplifying your life with this fun pin.

SIZE: $1\frac{1}{2}$" x $3\frac{3}{4}$"

MATERIALS:

idea-ology Trinkets
(Wings from Grungeboard Mixed Minis, Word Tag)
Ranger Adirondack Alcohol Ink
Pin Back
Cotton swab
E6000 Glue

INSTRUCTIONS:

1. Color Grungeboard wings with alcohol inks.
2. Glue word tag to wings.
3. Glue pin back in place.

Alcohol Ink on Board:
Squeeze 2 - 3 drops of alcohol ink onto a cotton swab. Rub alcohol ink onto Grungeboard.

'Memory' Key Brooch

Brooches have been worn by both men and women for centuries. Used to secure everything from cloaks and scarves to kilts, these striking pins make great fashion statements today.

see photo below

SIZE: $2\frac{1}{4}$" x $3\frac{1}{4}$"

MATERIALS:

idea-ology Trinkets: Key, Trinket Pin, Stencil Type, 1" Foliage Leaves, Link Chain, 5 Jump Rings
GS Hypo Cement,

INSTRUCTIONS:

1. Attach $2\frac{1}{2}$" of chain to key with jump rings.
2. Attach trinkets to chain links with jump rings.
3. Glue pin back in place.

Attach Chain to Key:
Attach chain to key with jump rings.

Attach Trinkets:
Attach trinkets and a pin with jump rings.